BROWN eyes

Holly McCain

Wasteland Press
Shelbyville, KY USA
www.wastelandpress.net

Brown Eyes
by Holly McCain

Copyright © 2007 Holly McCain
ALL RIGHTS RESERVED

First Printing – February 2007
ISBN13: 978-1-60047-081-3
ISBN10: 1-60047-081-5
Photos by Holly McCain

NO PART OF THIS BOOK MAY BE REPRODUCED IN ANY FORM, BY PHOTOCOPYING OR BY ANY ELECTRONIC OR MECHANICAL MEANS, INCLUDING INFORMATION STORAGE OR RETRIEVAL SYSTEMS, WITHOUT PERMISSION IN WRITING FROM THE COPYRIGHT OWNER/AUTHOR

Printed in the U.S.A.

ACKNOWLEDGMENTS

First, I would like to thank Bev for her insight. Bev, your thoughts were invaluable!

Special thanks as well to Betty, Mom of Shadow's Beau, Bear. Thank you for your encouragement and friendship. And thank you for bringing Bear into our lives.

An adoring thanks to my dear friend, Shirley. You were there to help me through it all! You understood my moods and were always there to give me a hug of encouragement.

I also need to give a BIG thanks to David and his Mom, Wanda. Thank you for letting me read my work in your home. Your input encouraged me to publish this book.

And another BIG thanks to my daughter, Beth for being there for me, and my grand daughter, Kylee, for her love of Shadow.

Thanks, too, to Chris for her kindness with Shadow and bringing Lucky into our lives, and to the many puppies and people whose lives have crossed paths with Shadow.

And the BIGGEST thanks to Shadow. This book would not have written without... you! We love you Shadow!

TABLE OF CONTENTS

My Friend	1
Shadow	3
Beau	5
Where did Our Puppy Come From?	6
Ma's Rules	9
Brown Eyes	10
Her Sister is a Cat	11
Soccer	13
Bath	14
Reflection	17
Serenity	18
The Dogs Next Door	20
Lucky	22
The Sweater	24
Tricks	25
Meeting Game	27
Sadie	28
Our Park	30
Shadow and Kylee	33
Sister Beth	34
Our Shadow	35
Shadow's Job	36
We Moved	38
Shadow's Pet ABC'S	40

My Friend

Clap your hands.
Stomp your feet.
Meet my friend.
My friend so neat!

She has brown eyes.
She has black hair.
Her ears are small.
She snores like a bear!

She has a yellow raincoat.
She has a sweater or two.
She doesn't own a pair of underwear.
I promise you!

She likes to play ball.
She likes to wear my hat.
She doesn't have to go to school.
What do you think of that?

She doesn't drink out of a cup.
She doesn't eat from a plate.
She has no hands.
My friend's so great!

She's not a mule.
She's not a hog.
She's not a goat.
She's not a frog.

She's not a bird.
She's not a cat.
She's not turtle.
She's not a bat.

Clap your hands.
Stomp your feet.
Don't read ahead.
Please don't cheat!

My friend's name is Shadow.
She's such a clown!
She makes me laugh.
She turns my frown upside down.

Do you give up?
Just yell YES!
My friend's a puppy dog.
Did you guess?

Shadow

Shadow's black and white.
Her ears hang low.
She's my best friend.
And I love her so.

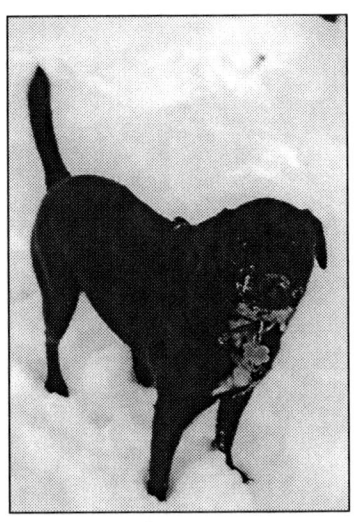

Her nose is short.
It's quite wet.
It holds many drops of water.
This I bet!

Her eyes seem sad.
She gets many treats.
I know you'd give in.
If you two ever did meet.

Her hair is black.
Her teeth are white.
She loves the snow.
She doesn't bite.

She likes to lick.
This is true.
That's how puppy dogs give kisses.
And how they say, "I love you."

Shadow's my best friend.
She's my pal.
She might be a puppy dog.
But she's one swell gal!

Beau

There's a puppy dog down the street.
He and Shadow like to meet.
He has blond hair.
The guy's name is Bear.

I swear he's Shadows' beau
They kiss, did you know?
He likes to smell her little butt.
I believe the guys a little nut!

He should watch his little nose.
He should watch where it goes.
I think he should keep it in the air.
Away from her butt I declare!

There's a puppy dog down the street.
He and Shadow bark when they meet.
They are quite a pair.
Shadow and her beau Bear.

Where did our puppy come from?

Do you know where our puppy dog came from?
She didn't grow in Ma's tummy.
She didn't come from a stork.
No, Shadow and storks weren't chummy.

Did she come from a pet store?
No, a pet store is out!
She didn't come with a receipt.
No. No pet store I shout!

Did I get her from a garage sale?
No, she wasn't someone's used stuff.
She didn't come from a garage sale.
No garage sale! Enough!

Did I get her from a neighbor?
No. No neighbor I say!
She didn't come from a neighbor.
No neighbor! No, way!

Did we buy her from a catalog?
No, she wasn't delivered by mail.
She didn't come from a postman or a pet store.
No neighbor or garage sale.

Did she come to us by airplane?
No, she didn't come by airplane, boat or train.
She didn't come from high up in the air.
No stork or airplane. You're being such a pain!

Did she come from a flea market?
Yes, she came from where people sell their ware!
There were apples, peaches and tools.
Toys and lots of stuff I swear!

She was in a car trunk.
Her siblings and she did share.
They all had their own charm.
She was like, "Touch me if you dare!"

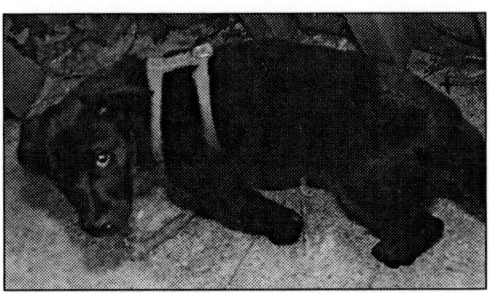

She lay hidden by each body.
Hers was the smallest one.
I wanted all of them.
We would've all had such fun!

Ma told me to pick only one.
So, one there would be.
She was the cutest!
The little girl was for me!

She didn't come with instructions,
on how to poop or pee.
She didn't wear a diaper.
We trained her you see!

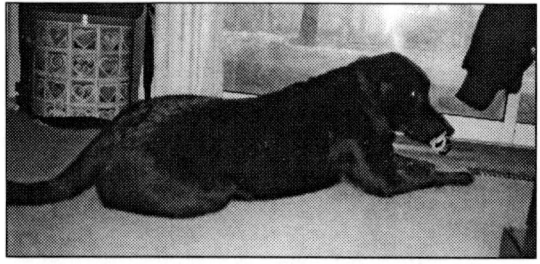

Where did our puppy dog come from?
I believe from God I'd say.
She fit in our house just right.
Yes, just right that February day!

Ma's Rules

She told her not to chase the cats.
She told her not to eat our hats.
She told her not to chew our shoes...
but what are puppy dogs suppose to do?

Cats sneak up on chairs.
Cats tease puppy dogs with their dares.
And if a hat lay by her drink,
It's hers don't you think?

Ma's rules are quite fine.
But they don't agree with hers or mine.
We say finder's keeper should be the rule.
God didn't create puppy dog fools!

Brown Eyes

Brown eyes stamped on our tomato plant.
Brown eyes tore up my fancy pants.
Brown eyes made Ma cuss and swear.
She tore up her underwear.
Brown eyes barked at the mailman.
Brown eyes pooped near the garbage can.
Brown eyes made Ma cuss and swear.
I saw her slobber in nice clean hair.
Brown eyes kissed Ma on the face.
In the living lay the broken vase.
Brown eyes made Ma laugh and cheer.
Brown eyes is our puppy dear
Brown eyes licked me when I was sad.
Brown eyes can't be so bad!

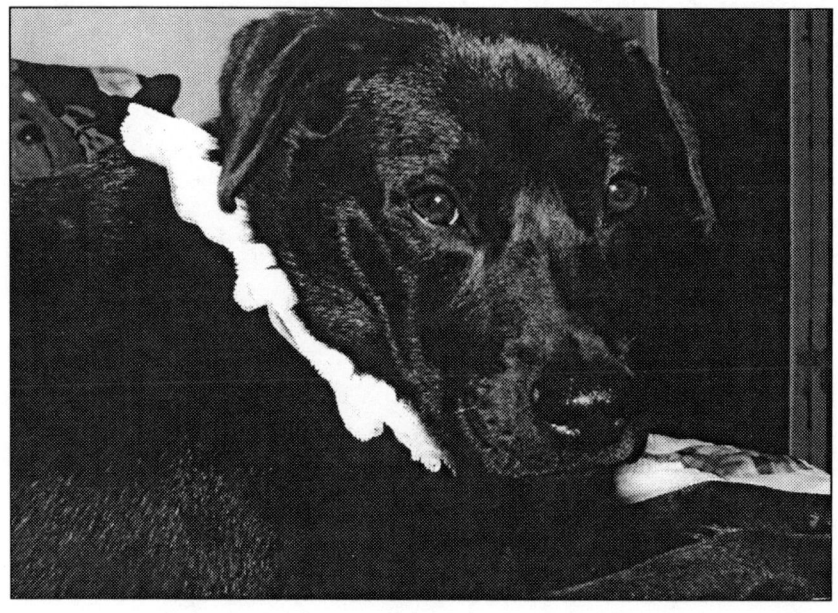

Her Sister is a Cat

What would her puppy dog friends say?
If they were to come to our house today!
If they saw her sister was a cat.
What do you think they'd think of that?

Would they laugh and roll around?
Would they look at her and grin and frown?
Would they whisper in each others ear?
"A cat for sister, she's nuts I fear!"

They would laugh right out our door.
Maybe leave a puddle on our floor.
Ma would yell this I know.
Please believe me, because this is so!

What would her puppy dog friends say?
If they were to come to our house today!
When they saw her brothers were birds.
There would be more puddles. Believe these words!

Soccer

I know Shadow loves to play soccer.
I'm sure this is true.
She loves to play night or day.
Whether the balls white or blue!

She puts her little paw on the ball.
She holds it just right.
Please don't try to take it.
She'd fight you will all her might!

I know Shadow loves to play soccer.
She plays whether it's cold or hot.
She puts her paw on the ball.
And smiles with all she's got!

I know Shadow loves to play soccer.
I do believe it's so.
Or why would she waiting for you and me.
She's like, "Come on let's go!"

Bath

Puppy dogs need a bath. That's ma's firmest rule.
This is a fight. A people and puppy duel.

We must get Shadow into the tub first you see.
She may hide from Ma and me.

She might hide under a bed.
She might be behind a chair or have a cover over her head.

We must hunt here and there.
Shadow could be anywhere.

She could be hiding with the cat.
She could be near my baseball hat.

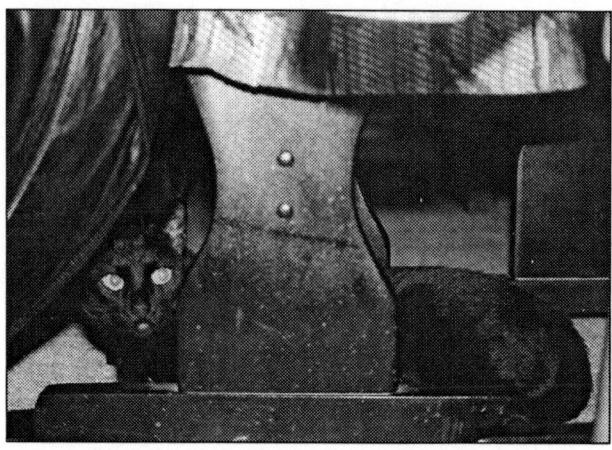

She could be near the back door.
She could even be on the kitchen floor.

I know she couldn't be in the bird cage up high.
She is special, but everyone knows a dog can't fly!

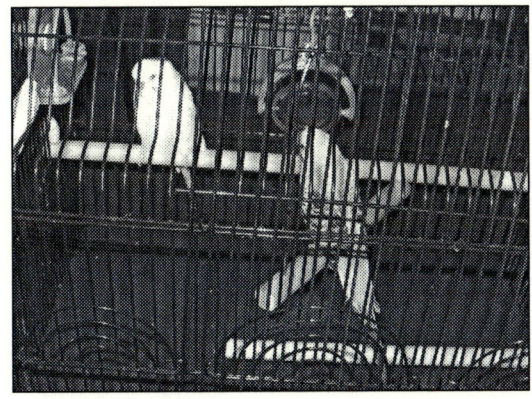

I know she's not with her beau Bear.
I didn't let her out. I swear!

Is she in her puppy dog bed?
That has covers white and red.

Shadow can be such a ham!
She's hiding there with little lamb.

We must lift her into the tub.
Now we're determined to give this puppy dog more then a scrub.

First, we wet her fur, one time or two.
Second, we soap her with shampoo.

Third, we rinse her off once or twice.
Fourth, we dry her. She smells so nice!

She shakes the water from her hair.
The water goes everywhere.

Now that wasn't so bad. Shadow's now clean and sweet.
But ma and I are wet from head to feet!

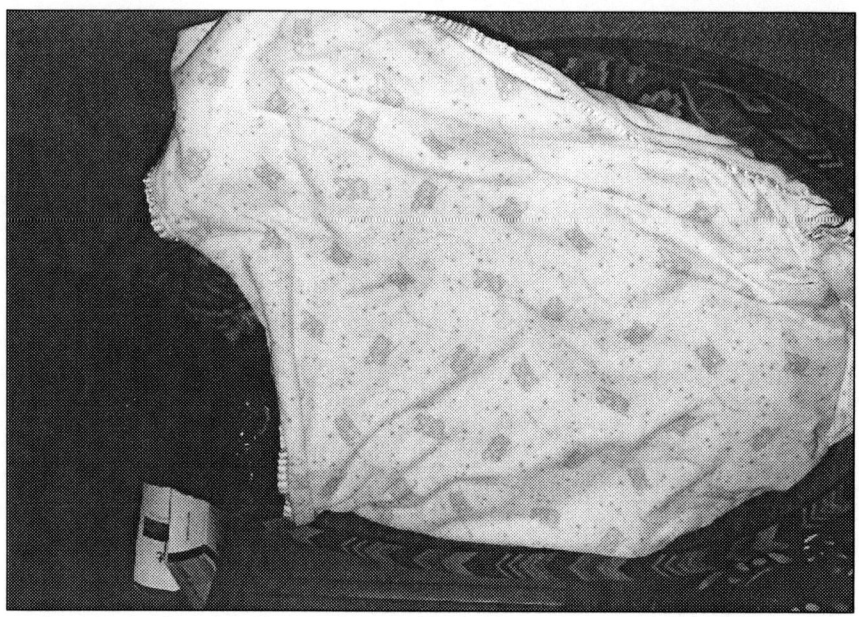

Reflection

Shadow saw her reflection in the mirror today.
Was she afraid, I couldn't say!
She barked so loud I do fear.
My ears have lost their will to hear.

Shadow saw her reflection in a mirror again.
It was so hard not to laugh or grin.
She peeked once or twice.
Can you give me your advice?

What do I do or say?
How do I explain in a puppy dog way?
Please hurry and tell me what to do!
She thinks it's another puppy dog I'm telling you!.

Maybe she thinks its Sue, Jim or Mack.
She waits for it to bark right back.
She's been waiting night and day.
She dares that mirror to go away.

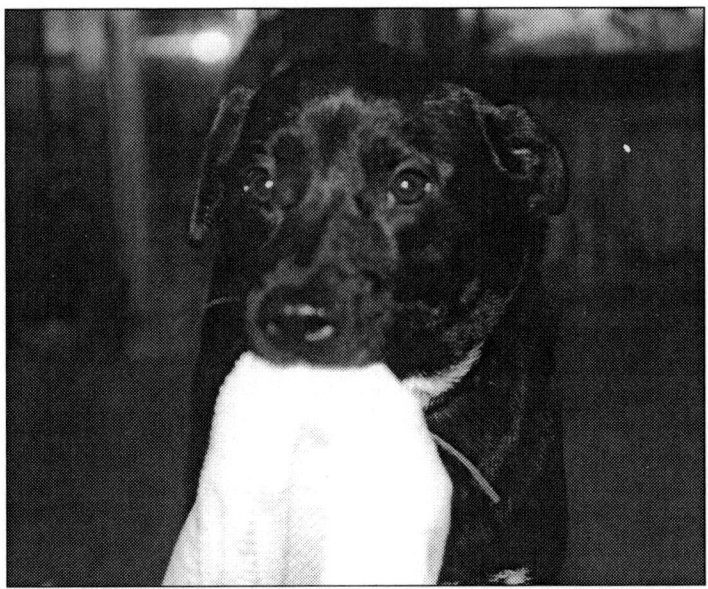

Serenity

She was Shadows pal.
They liked to play.
Hide-and-seek
Night or day

Serenity would tag Shadow.
Then run around.
She would hide,
Until she was found

The game continued until both were tired.
Then on to the couch they'd lay.
Resting, together
Until again, they'd play

This went on for six years.
The cat would hide.
Here comes puppy dog!
Down the hall she'd slide!

They played thousands of minutes.
Of hide and chase
Those two friends
Were all over the place!

Dodging people and the other cat
Who didn't understand, and would get mad.
"A cat and a puppy dog for friends!"
"Oh!" She'd nod her head and look so sad!

She didn't understand.
She thought they were a strange pair.
That cat and puppy dog
On the living room chair

Didn't they know they were different?
One was a cat.
One was a puppy dog.
On the chair the two sat.

She was Shadows pal.
They liked to play.
Shadow misses Serenity.
She's in heaven today.

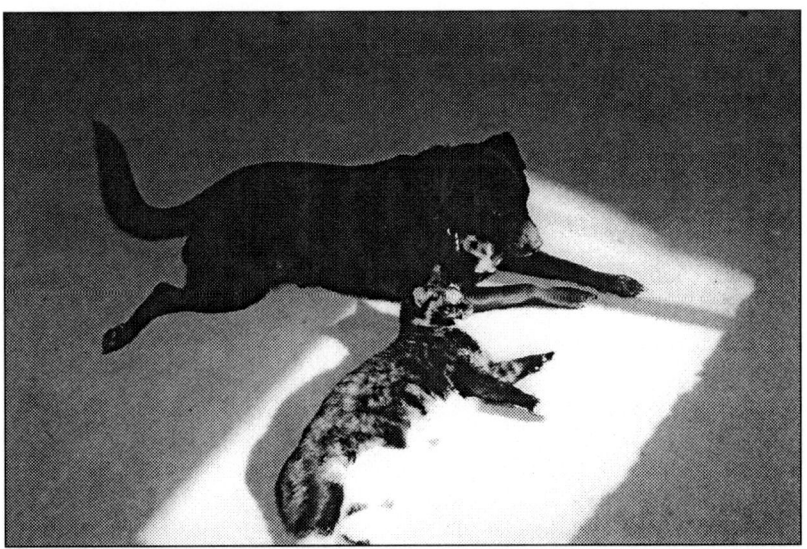

The Dogs Next Door

There are two dogs next door.
They are Shadow's friends.
Are they good neighbors?
Well, it all depends!

They are both small.
They both have loud squeaks.
They sound like two cats,
in a fight at high peak!

They try to warn Shadow.
Their squeak is a bark.
They squeak night and day.
Even when it's dark!

They give that loud yelp.
It's like they say.
"Shadow please come out."
"Something's not right today."

It could be a dog.
It could be a cat.
It could be a mailman.
A mailman with a mailman hat!

It could be car.
It could be anything on our street.
They are the neighborhood patrol.
They are out on their beat!

They are Shadow's two friends.
They are dogs next door.
They are on neighborhood patrol.
 Hear them roar!

Lucky

She lived on the corner of our fence.
She was a dog of a different breed.
Her name was Lucky.
She was lucky indeed!

She lived with her mom.
My story is true.
She got lots of love.
A daily hug or two

She was Shadow's friend.
They'd meet at the fence.
Shadow would try to get her to run.
Back and forth it was real intense!

Lucky would look at Shadow.
She must have thought she was crazy.
Shadow would run back and forth.
The puppy dog was sure not lazy!

Lucky's mom said she was old.
No, Shadow didn't believe.
She'd go back and forth.
The puppy dog wouldn't leave!

She wasn't just Shadow's friend.
She was one our family I'd say.
We miss Lucky.
She is with God today.

We miss her Doberman eyes.
We miss her Sheppard bark.
We now only see,
the worn out grass where she did park.

This poem is for Lucky.
She was Shadow's friend for many years.
We miss her gentle eyes.
They gave us many smiles and tears.

The Sweater

We bought Shadow a sweater.
It is made of fleece.
It is purple.
It is one full piece.

It has colorful trim.
It fits her just right.
It can warm her knees.
She looks dynamite!

I put it on her.
She struggled to get free.

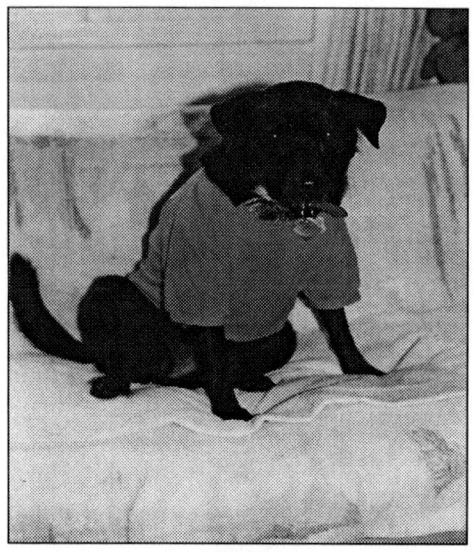

She even ignored my pets.
She walked away from me!

Today it's warmer.
Naked she'll be.
No purple sweater.
Only fur for she!

Tricks

My puppy dog Shadow.
Does tricks on the spot.
She can pick the hand which holds the treat.
But sometimes it's not!

She can find me when I hide.
Yes, before you can count to three.
And now you may be quite impressed.
But, she does more. Just listen to me!

I ask for five dollars.
Her little paw touches my hand.
She'll give me much more.
But I think five is just grand!

She'll roll over.
She'll shake my hand.
She'll sit.
She'll stand.

She'll pick up a towel.
She'll bring me a ball.
She'll show me her tummy.
She'll kiss me when I fall.

HOLLY McCAIN

She'll move over on the couch.
Ring the bell when she needs to go out.
Knock when it's time to come in.
Come to me when I shout.

My puppy dog Shadow.
She does many tricks its true.
Yes, I'm proud.
That's why I'm telling you.

Meeting Game

Shadow's friends like to meet her at the door.
Together they roll and play on the floor.
They smell or lick each other's face.
And take over our people space.

Outside, they sniff each pole and tree.
They look for messages left, you see.
We humans might complain.
I guess we think these meetings are insane.

A message could be a glance.
Or a jumping dance.
It may be a bark from delight.
Or a growl with all their might!

Shadow and all puppies like to meet.
Whether, it's five below, or in the summer heat.
Our human life-styles aren't the same.
We're too intense to play the meeting game!

Sadie

We went to the pet store one day.
It was too rainy to walk our block.
Yes, the puddles were so deep.
They would've filled my brand new socks.

We saw leashes, collars, toys and beds.
We looked at birds, rats, and fish of all kinds.
We sure didn't know our lives would change.
On the last aisle a new sister we'd find.

She was in the middle of the floor.
Jumping and dancing a jig.
We asked about her size.
They didn't know just how big.

Her mom was a Sheppard.
Her dad was a Greyhound.
She was tall for her age.
Oh, how that girl could get around!

Shadow kept glancing at the puppy.
She didn't look with dread.
She knew she'd be sharing her territory.
Not a one puppy home. Two instead!

She looked like a Sadie.
So, Sadie she'd be.
Shadow's little sister.
Yes, more walks for me!

Life has changed at our house.
Now two puppy dogs share my bed.
Sometimes Shadow seems to look at us like,
"Did you two have something loose in your head?"

Our Park

We are off to our park.
She wants to smell each fire hydrant we embark.
She tries to persuade me to chase a cat.
I say, "No," to that!

Shadow walks with such pride.
She's my little guide.
She shows me poles, flowers and bees.
All Gods treasures she helps me see.

Our park is our favorite place.
There she can have her space.
I let her jump and run.
Shadow and I, just having fun!

There's a pond at our park.
In it are ducks, geese and even tree bark.
We walk around it once or twice.
Watching the birds is so nice!

She wants to go up on the slide.
The park rules won't abide.
The sign says, "No pets."
So, we're off to the basketball nets.

I bend to throw the ball.
Shadow races to it before it falls.
It doesn't get in the net.
It's Shadows' point I bet!

I try to dribble the ball.
Shadow calls it her call.
She hits it with her paw.
I just yell, "Aw!"

Shadow wins the game.
When we play it's always the same.
She's much too fast.
But she and I have a blast!

We now climb the park hill.
Up there the views even better still!
We can see more birds in the trees.
Now we must go. Shadow needs to pee.

We go to the grass.
She lets out some gas.
She finds her spot.
When you have to go, it's much better then not!

Now we can jump the poles.
Can we believe we both never fall?
We only jump the ones our height.
We jumped a new one with delight!

Now it's time to walk away.
It's time go home, not time to play.
We look both ways at each street.
Stop at the red light that we meet.

When we're home and in the door,
I give her a treat or two or four.
Now Shadow puts her head down on my knee.
Shadow and I rest. We're tired you see.

Shadow and Kylee

She giggled when she barked.
She laughed when she licked.
She smiled when their eyes met.
Shadow and Kylee are thick.

She crawled after her tail.
She gave her a bite of her cheese.
They shook hands.
Shadow and Kylee are like flowers and honey bees.

They play on the slide.
They run through the grass.
They play fetch.
Shadow and Kylee's friendship is first-class.

Sister Beth

She has a few sisters.
Yes, three in all.
But one of her favorites,
is the one who can throw a ball.

She has long hair.
She walks on two feet.
They don't look alike.
She doesn't jump when they meet.

She eats with a fork.
She sips with a straw.
She pets Shadow on the head.
She's a human, that's her only flaw.

She wears pants.
She doesn't have paws for feet.
She never licks her plate.
She uses a knife to cut her meat.

Beth is a human.
Shadow is a puppy dog.
They're sisters.
Hey, at least Shadow's not a skunk or hog!

Our Shadow

People can't buy loyalty.
No matter if they're one or one hundred and two.
People can't buy friendship.
One that's tried and true.

People can't buy love.
No matter if they're rich or poor.
People can't buy a guide.
Who is a friend and more!

Ma and I have all of this.
She came into our life one February day.
She is our Shadow.
Now clap and yell hurray!

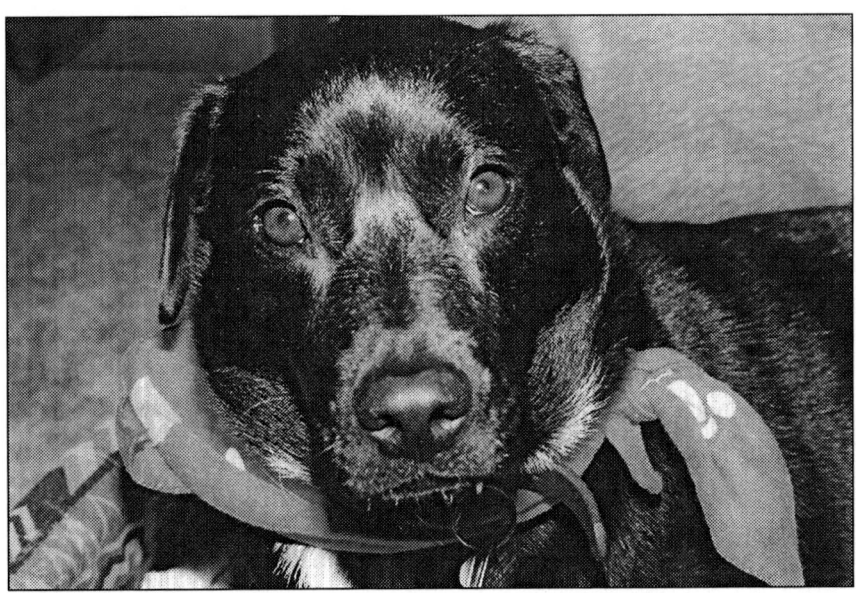

Shadow's Job

Shadow's job is to be by my side.
And give me a lick or two.
My job is to reward her.
I give her a good-old human thank-you.

I cuddle her nice and close.
That's what I do.
'Cause I love my puppy dog.
I even love her if her mouth smells like the zoo.

She might have drunk from the toilet.
She might have licked her little butt.
I still love her.
And I say, "so what!"

I can hold my breath.
And cuddle her close to me.
'Cause I love my puppy dog.
She means the world to me.

She may roll in the yard.
Yes, roll in globs of nasty stuff.
My job is to reward her.
Because my Shadow's good enough!

Shadow's job is to be my puppy dog.
And she's great at that!
I don't care how she smells.
'Cause she's magnificent!

We Moved

We've moved into a new home.
One built for us from scratch.
I know Shadow's first home was special.
But, this one we've become attached.

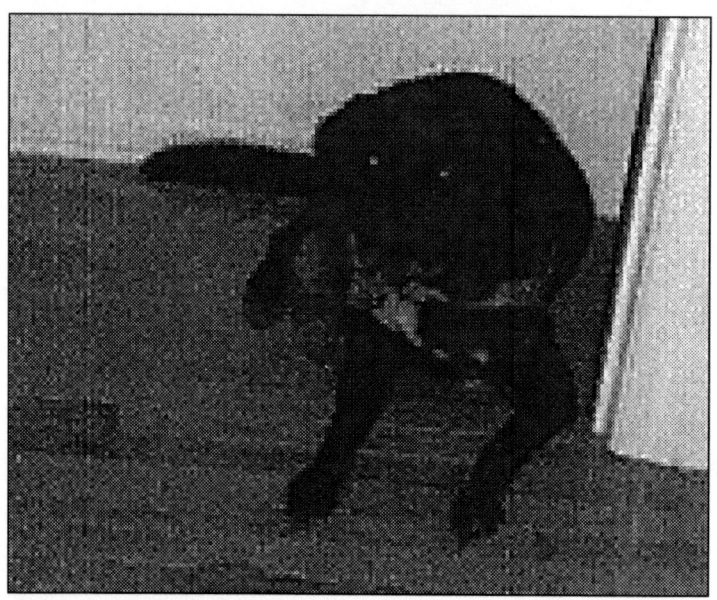

We can play in the basement.
We can walk on paths.
We can play on the playground.
"There are 'No Pet' signs", I laugh.

We'll miss the old house.
Its memories will last our whole life through.
It was special.
It kept us warm this is true.

It was a good home.
This I know.
It housed all of us.
But it was just time for us to go.

Shadow and I still visit.
We clean and close all ties.
I hope someone will move in that loves it.
It was just time for us to say good-bye.

One thing about moving,
memories won't leave or go away.
My first eight years with Shadow,
are always in my heart to stay.

Shadow's Pet ABC's

Now you are about to close this book up tight.
I'll tell you how to pass the day and night.
I'll whisper it in your ear.
And nobody will overhear.

No one will dare intrude.
I believe their ears would grow big.
Maybe they'd look like an elephant or pig.

Please don't let them sneak right up.
That would make me all shook-up.
Now please listen to me.
Before I squirm and pee.

This book was about loyalty, trust and devotion.

It's about laughter, crying and deep emotion.
It's about a brown-eyed puppy that's close to my heart.
A bet you loved her from the start!

Now listen real well.
Like a good girl or boy should.
If you have a puppy, cat, bird, turtle or any pet.
Please read out loud Shadow's pet alphabet.

A, B, C, D, E, F, G,
How a pet makes my days pass like a jamboree.
H, I, J, K, L, M, N, O, P,
They like to cuddle, walk and even play Frisbee.

Q, R, S, T, U, V,
Pets show us love I guarantee.
W, X, Y and Z,
Now I'm done saying Shadow's pet ABC's.

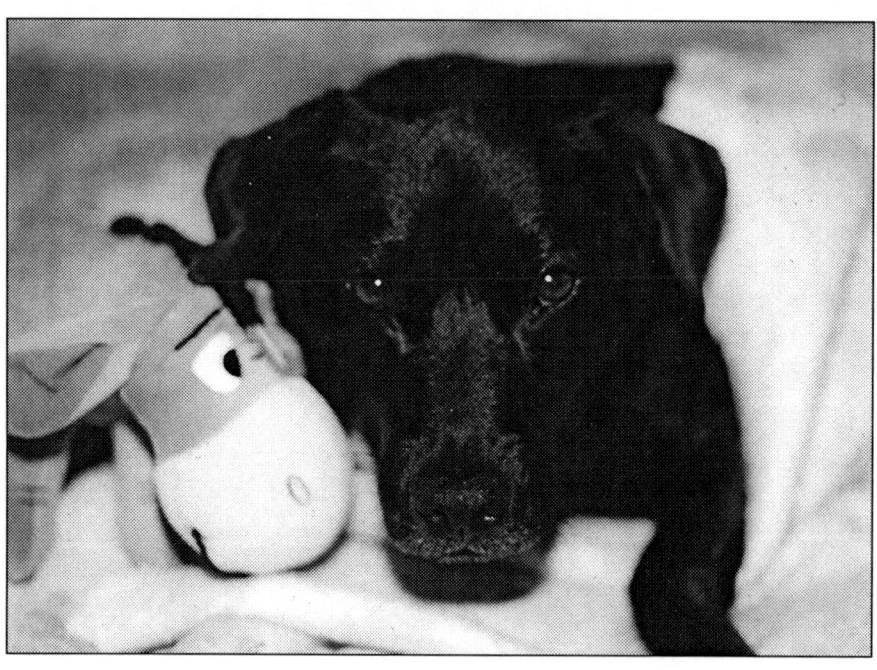

Printed in the United States
75775LV00007B/235-240